## DATE DUE

|  |  |  |  |
|---|---|---|---|
|  |  |  |  |
|  |  |  |  |
|  |  |  |  |
|  |  |  |  |
|  |  |  |  |
|  |  |  |  |
|  |  |  |  |
|  |  |  |  |
|  |  |  |  |
|  |  |  |  |
|  |  |  |  |
|  |  |  |  |

# Fun
# Experiments

## with

# Matter

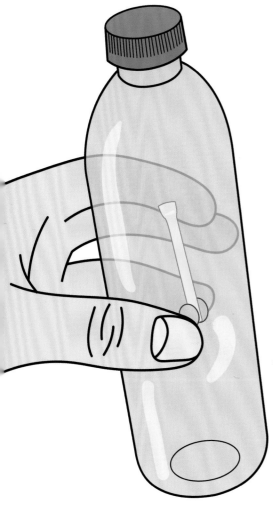

Thanks to the creative team:
Senior Editor: Alice Peebles
Fact checking: Tom Jackson
Design: www.collaborate.agency

Hungry Tomato®
A division of Lerner Publishing Group, Inc.
241 First Avenue North
Minneapolis, MN 55401 USA

For reading levels and more information, look up this title at www.lernerbooks.com.

Main body text set in Minya Nouvelle Regular 12/15.

**Library of Congress Cataloging-in-Publication Data**

The Cataloging-in-Publication Data for *Fun Experiments with Matter: Invisible Ink, Giant Bubbles, and More* is on file at the Library of Congress.
ISBN 978-1-5124-3216-9 (lib. bdg.)
ISBN 978-1-5124-4997-6 (EB pdf)

Manufactured in the United States of America
1-41771-23532-4/6/2017

# Fun Experiments

## with

# Matter

by Rob Ives
Illustrated by Eva Sassin

HUNGRY TOMATO®
Minneapolis

# Safety First

Take care and use good sense with these amazing science experiments—some are very simple, while others are trickier.

Each project includes a list of everything you will need. Most of the items are things you can find around the house, or they are things that are readily available and inexpensive to buy.

Be sure to check out the Amazing Science behind the projects and learn the scientific principles involved in each experiment.

Watch for this sign throughout the book. You may need help from an adult to complete these tasks.

4

# Contents

# Matter

Matter is everything in the universe that's not just empty space. Even though most of the universe is empty space, there's still an awful lot of matter—enough to make a solid ball stretching all the way to the nearest star and back!

Matter comes in three main forms: solid, liquid, and gas. These are called states of matter, and they may seem very different. But matter can actually switch from one state to the other and back if the temperature and pressure are right. Your body is made from a mix of all three states of matter.

You'll learn how to make giant bubbles, cornstarch that bounces, a superpowered fountain, and much more. Matter matters. . . .

## You will need:

Cornstarch

Sugar

2-liter bottle of diet cola

Liquid dish soap

Clear plastic 500mL drink bottle

Glycerine    Food coloring

Baking powder

Plastic folder

Masking tape    Coffee stirrers x2

Clothespins x2    Wooden skewers x4

Water-soluble felt-tip pens

Small container

Lemon

Cotton swabs

Unlined paper

Tea lights x2

Large paper clips x3

3 feet (1 m) thick string or yarn

Citric acid

BAKING SODA
200g

POWDERED SUGAR

15-inch-long (40 cm) ⁷⁄₈-inch (22 mm) round dowel x2

Washer

Baking soda

Powdered sugar

Bendy plastic drinking straws x13

White coffee filter papers

Flavored gelatin or jelly crystals

Chewy mints

10 feet (3 m) string

Thumb tacks x2

Small bowls x2

Small glass jar

# What tools will I need?

Saucepan

Pliers

Scissors

Shallow tray

Stapler

Gaffer tape (or duct tape)

Large jug

Cup

Butter knife

Pencil

Measuring spoons

# Cartesian Diver

This clever toy, invented by French thinker René Descartes, features a tiny diving tube in a bottle. The "diver" sinks when the bottle is squeezed. The pressure from your hand makes it move—relax your hand and up it pops!

Tea light

Thumb tacks x2

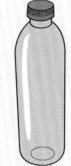

Clear plastic 500mL drink bottle

Plastic drinking straw

### Tools you will need:
#### (see page 7)

✴ Butter knife  ✴ Scissors

---

Do not place fingers, clothing, or any other materials near the flame. Extinguish the flame immediately upon completing the experiment.

**1.** Heat the end of the straw so that it just starts to melt.

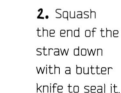

**2.** Squash the end of the straw down with a butter knife to seal it.

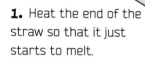

**3.** Trim the straw at the other end with scissors to roughly 1.5 to 2 inches (4–5 cm) in length.

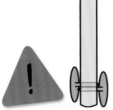

**5.** Fill the bottle with water right up to the top.

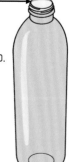

**4.** Push a drawing pin in from each side of the straw at the open end. These act as weights so that the straw floats upright.

8

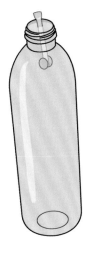

**6.** Drop the diver into the water. A few millimeters of straw should be above the surface of the water. If the diver sticks out a long way, shorten the straw. If it sinks into the water right away, start again with a longer section of straw.

**7.** Fit the lid on the bottle and screw it down tight.

# Squeeze the bottle to control the diver!

## Amazing Science

*Water cannot be squeezed, or compressed, into a smaller space, but air can be. When you squeeze the bottle, the air in the diver takes up less space. The diver then takes in water, becomes more dense, and sinks.*

# Bubble Mix

## You will need:

This bubble recipe only needs ingredients from the kitchen cupboard. The cornstarch and glycerine add to its strength. Prepare it and use it for the next two experiments, which show how water can be made to hold pockets of air—quite big ones too!

1 teaspoon baking powder

1 tablespoon gycerine

2 tablespoons cornstarch

½ cup liquid dish soap

### Tools you will need:
(see page 7)

✴ Cup ✴ Measuring spoons ✴ Large jug

**1.** Add 2 tablespoons of cornstarch to an 8-ounce cup.

**2.** Start adding the water a little at a time. Stir it while you add, and continue until the cup is full.

**3.** Add the mixture to a large jug. Then add two more cups of water and stir to mix.

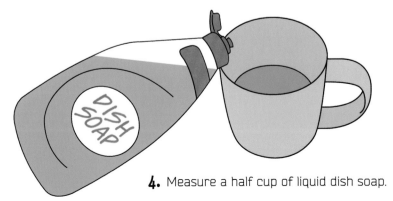

**4.** Measure a half cup of liquid dish soap.

**5.** Add the dish soap to the mix.

**6.** Add 1 tablespoon of glycerine.

**7.** Add 1 teaspoon of baking powder.

**8.** Mix thoroughly. Be careful not to create bubbles. The bubble mix works best when not covered in a foam.

## Amazing Science

When water is mixed with soap, the soap weakens its surface tension. Surface tension is the attraction between water molecules, which pulls the water together into a droplet. When surface tension is reduced, air can move in to form a bubble.

# Big Bubbles

Using the bubble mix recipe from pp. 10–11, you can take a giant step forward in bubble-making with this experiment.

## You Will need:

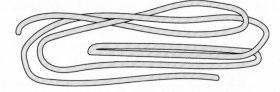

3-foot-long (1-m) thick string or yarn

15-inch-long (40 cm ) 7/8-inch (22 mm) round dowel x2

### Tools you Will need:
(see page 7)

✮Pliers

Gaffer tape
(or duct tape)

Large paper clips x2

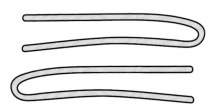

**1.** Use pliers to help you unfold the paper clips, and then re-fold them into a U shape.

**2.** Hold a paper clip over the end of each stick to make a loop and tape it in place.

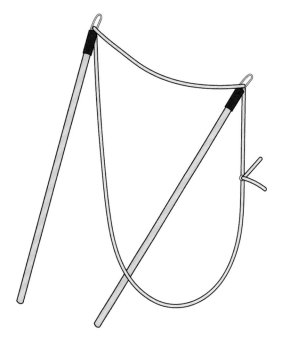

**3.** Thread the string through the loops at the ends of the sticks. Tie the string ends to make a loop.

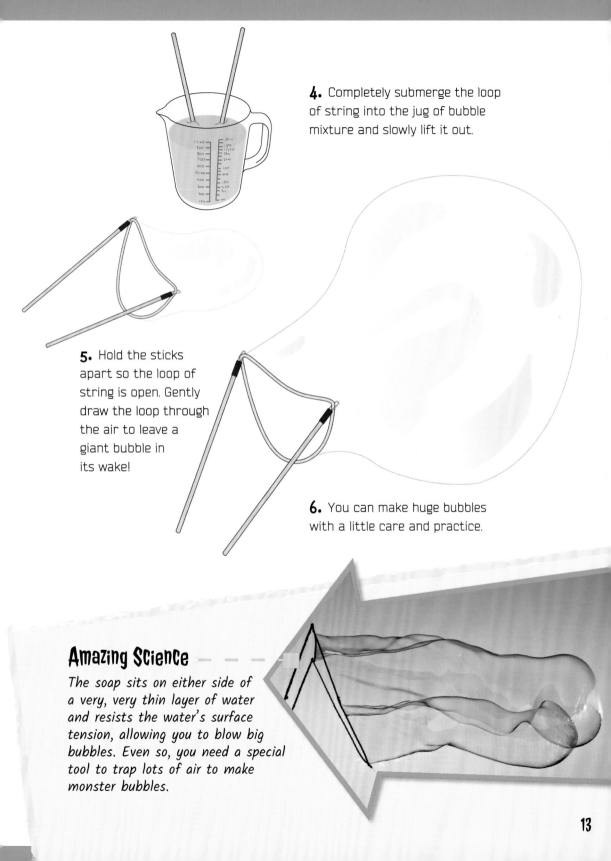

**4.** Completely submerge the loop of string into the jug of bubble mixture and slowly lift it out.

**5.** Hold the sticks apart so the loop of string is open. Gently draw the loop through the air to leave a giant bubble in its wake!

**6.** You can make huge bubbles with a little care and practice.

## Amazing Science

*The soap sits on either side of a very, very thin layer of water and resists the water's surface tension, allowing you to blow big bubbles. Even so, you need a special tool to trap lots of air to make monster bubbles.*

# Bubble Cube

Want a change from round bubbles? Again, use the mix from pp. 10–11. This time, construct a cube frame to make a big bubble that mirrors its straight-sided shape.

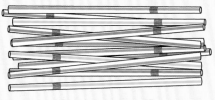

Bendy straws x12

Wooden skewers x4

## Tools you will need:
(see page 7)

✯ Scissors

**1.** Bend a straw to a 90-degree angle.

**2.** Squish the short end of each straw so it will fit into another straw.

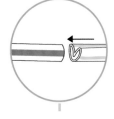

**3.** Fit four straws together like this to make a square.

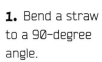

**4.** Repeat the process to make a second square.

14

**5.** Cut the bendy sections off four more straws and discard.

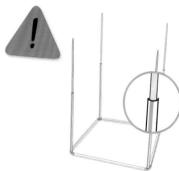

**6.** Push a wooden skewer through the corner of one of the squares.

**7.** Repeat on all the other corners. Push them up to be even with the straw square.

**8.** Slip the four cut-off straws over the skewers.

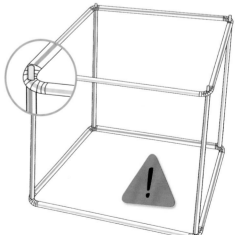

**9.** Push the second square down over the skewers.

**10.** Keep pushing the square down until it rests on the four straws.

**11.** Trim off the ends of the skewers with scissors.

**12.** Pour bubble mix into a tray. Dip the cube into the mix and rotate it so that each face is immersed. Lift the cube out.

**13.** A cube-shaped bubble will be suspended between the faces. You may need to give it a couple of tries!

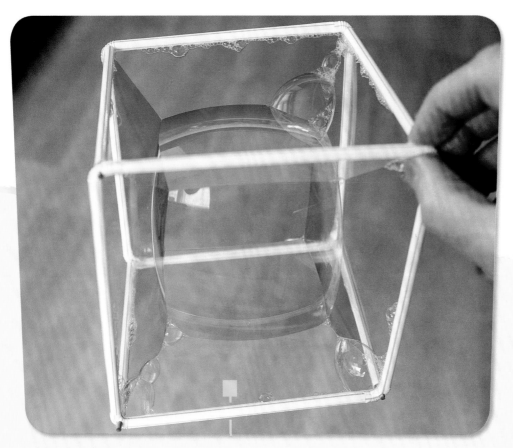

## Amazing Science

*Floating bubbles are naturally round because that shape keeps them most stable—the surface area of a sphere is the smallest (and strongest) for enclosing the maximum amount of air. But bubbles can also mirror geometric structures, such as this cube shape which allows for a minimal surface area.*

# Cornstarch Slime

## You will need:

2 Small bowls

Water

CORN STARCH
3 tablespoons cornstarch

Cornstarch is a fascinating material. When mixed with water in the correct proportions, it becomes what is known as a non-Newtonian fluid. This has some really weird properties!

## Tools you will need:
(see page 7)

✷Measuring spoons

**1.** Add 3 tablespoons of cornstarch to one bowl. Add water a little at a time, mixing it gently to form a thick paste.

**2.** Time to experiment! Pour the mix from one bowl to another. It will flow smoothly just like any normal liquid.

**3.** Now try stirring it with a spoon. If you stir it slowly, it will be just like any other liquid. But the faster you try to stir, the thicker and harder the mix becomes. If you move your spoon through the mix really fast, it becomes a solid and will even crack and break! Amazing!

## Amazing Science

*Most liquids splash or flow away if you hit them. But not cornstarch slime. Non-Newtonian fluids (see p. 30) don't act like a regular liquid. This slime can behave like a liquid or a solid. It locks solid when you hit it hard and flows if you push gently. That's because when you hit it, the water in the slime rushes away, leaving solid cornstarch.*

# Bouncy Ball

You Will need:

A few drops of food coloring

Water

**CORN STARCH**

3 tablespoons cornstarch

Here's another way to transform cornstarch—this time into a squishy object. Just add water, and then cook up your ball! Remember to keep your spoonfuls consistent.

**Tools you Will need:**
(see page 7)

☆ Measuring spoons
☆ Microwave

**1.** Mix 3 tablespoons of cornstarch and 1 tablespoon of water in a bowl. Add a drop or two of extra water if it doesn't mix completely.

**2.** Add a few drops of food coloring, and mix it in.

**3.** Microwave the mixture for 20 seconds. Mix in another teaspoon of water.

18

**4.** Roll the mixture into a ball between your palms.

**5.** Microwave the ball for 15 seconds

**6.** Let the ball cool completely, then give it a try!

## Amazing Science

*Not all solid substances are rigid. Some are elastic. They might stretch or squeeze under pressure but bounce back to their original shape. A rubber ball squishes out of shape when it hits the ground, then shoots itself up in the air as it regains its shape.*

19

# Separating Colors

A solution is a liquid in which substances are dissolved. The technique for separating out the colors in solutions is called chromatography. It is used here to find out which colors make up the inks in felt-tip pens. Dark colored pens work best!

## You Will need:

White coffee filter papers

Clothespins x2

Water-soluble felt-tip pens

Coffee stirrer

### Tools you Will need:
(see page 7)

☆ Shallow tray
☆ Scissors
☆ Stapler

**1.** Cut four thin strips from the coffee filter, all about 3 inches (70 mm) long.

**2.** Fold over the ends of each strip and staple it down. This will make a loop that the coffee stirrer fits through. Repeat with the other strips..

**3.** Choose four water-soluble felt-tip pens of different colors. Draw a line across each paper strip roughly 0.5 inches (15 mm) from the end of the strip.

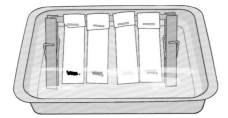

**4.** Repeat with the other three colors.

**5.** Thread the coffee stirrer through the ends of the strips

**6.** Make a frame with the two clothespins as shown.

**7.** Stand the frame in a shallow tray. Add water just to reach the bottom of the strips.

**8.** As the water soaks its way up the strips, it pulls the inks with it. Some colors move higher up the strips than others, which causes them to separate.

## Amazing Science

*The inks separate into their colors because they behave differently in contact with water. Different colors flow more easily than others and move further up the paper.*

# Growing Crystals

## You will need:

Bag of sugar

Small glass jar

String

1 mug of water

Metal washer

Coffee stirrer

Crystals are both fascinating and beautiful! You can grow your own with just a few household items. Here we grow sugar crystals, but you can also try using salt or baking powder in the same way.

## Tools you will need:
### (see page 7)

✷ Saucepan ✷ Spoon

Food coloring

**1.** Tie the washer to one end of a length of string. Tie the other end of string around the coffee stirrer.

**2.** Span the stick across the top of a jar. Adjust the string so that the washer hangs just above the bottom of the jar. Set aside.

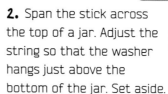

**3.** Boil a mug of water in a pan. Add sugar to the water, one spoonful at a time. Stir the water until the sugar is completely dissolved.

**4.** Keep adding sugar a spoonful at a time until no more will dissolve. This is known as a saturated solution. It will be quite syrupy. If you want colored crystals, you can add a few drops of food coloring.

**5.** Let the liquid cool and then pour it into the empty jar.

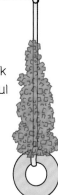

**7.** Now leave it on a shelf out of the way. In a week you'll find beautiful crystals have formed on the string.

**6.** Dangle your string into the solution.

## Amazing Science

Everything is made of tiny particles called atoms. Atoms form molecules. Crystals grow gradually as molecules join together. In a crystal, the joined atoms form regular, geometric shapes. Here, as water evaporates from the saturated sugar-water solution, sugar molecules are left behind. They collect on the string to form crystals.

23

# Invisible Ink

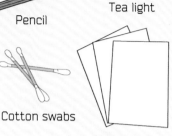

Pencil

Tea light

Send secret messages to your spy friends using your very own invisible ink.

Small container

½ lemon

Cotton swabs

Unlined paper

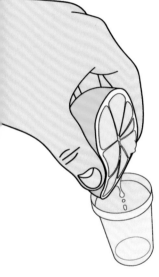

**1.** Squeeze some lemon juice into the container.

**2.** Mark out a rectangle in pencil on the paper for your message. The ink really is invisible, and this will show you where you've written.

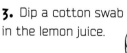

**3.** Dip a cotton swab in the lemon juice.

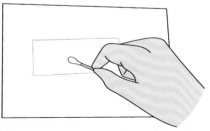

**4.** Write your message in lemon juice inside the rectangle. Keep dipping the cotton swab in the lemon juice to keep it "charged."

**5.** Let the message dry completely.

**6.** Reveal the message by holding the paper above a burning tea light. Be careful!

! Do not place fingers, clothing, or any other materials near the flame. Extinguish the flame immediately upon completing the experiment.

## The heat from the candle will darken the dried lemon juice, revealing your secret message!

### Amazing Science

*Normally, lemon juice is almost transparent. But if you heat it, the juice reacts with oxygen in the air and turns brown. This is called oxidation. It is an example of a chemical reaction—the change that occurs in chemicals when they meet. Rust is the oxidation of iron when it meets air and water, as you can see with the can on the right.*

# Fizzy Sweets

3 teaspoons powdered sugar

2 teaspoons baking soda

1 package flavored gelatin or jelly crystals

Make your own fizzy candy powder, and learn what gives it fizz!

Small bowl

2 teaspoons citric acid

**Tools you will need:**
(see page 7)

✴ Measuring spoons

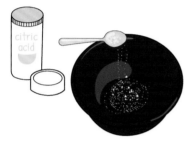

**1.** Measure 2 teaspoons of citric acid into a bowl.

**2.** Add 2 teaspoons of baking soda and mix together. These are the two ingredients that give the candy its fizz. When they mix with the saliva in your mouth, they react just like an effervescent tablet dropped in water.

**3.** Add 3 teaspoons of powdered sugar to sweeten the mix. Add a tablespoon of flavored gelatin to flavor your fizzy candy powder. Mix the ingredients thoroughly.

**Your fizzy candy is now ready to try—pop a little on your tongue. Tasty!**

 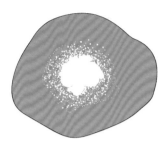 

**4.** To pack your fizzy candy powder as a gift for a friend, cut out circles of tissue.

**5.** Add a little powder to the middle of each circle.

## Twist!

## Amazing Science

*Sherbet is a sweet that gives you a fizzing sensation if you put it on your tongue. The fizzing is a chemical reaction. The saliva in your mouth dissolves citric acid crystals in the fizzy candy powder. The citric acid reacts with the baking soda to make tiny bubbles of carbon dioxide gas.*

# Spring Fountain

A remote-controlled fountain made from diet cola and chewy mints really packs a pop!

## You will need:

Chewy mints

Large paper clip

10 feet (3 m) string

DIET COLA
2-liter bottle of diet cola

Plastic folder

Sticky tape

### Tools you will need:
(see page 7)

✷ Pliers  ✷ Scissors

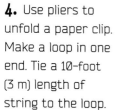

**1.** Cut one side from the plastic folder and roll it into a tube.

**2.** Make sure it will fit tightly in the neck of the bottle. Secure with a couple of strips of sticky tape.

**3.** Make a hole on either side of the tube with the point of a pair of scissors. ➞

**4.** Use pliers to unfold a paper clip. Make a loop in one end. Tie a 10-foot (3 m) length of string to the loop.

**5.** Fit the paper clip through the holes in the plastic tube. This will be your release mechanism to trigger the reaction!

**6.** Remove the tube, keeping the pin in place, and fill it with chewy mints from the top.

## 7. Now go outside!

Open the bottle and fit the tube securely into the neck. Stand at a safe distance holding the end of the string.

# 3...2...1...
# ...pull the string!

**8.** The mints are released into the cola and—whoosh!— the drink shoots out of the bottle like a fizzy fountain!

## Amazing Science

*The soda is bubbly because it is full of carbon dioxide gas. The mints have tiny dimples on their surface which make bubbles form fast. When the mints are dropped in with the soda all at once, they create an explosive effect.*

# Glossary

**chromatography:** A technique for separating the dissolved substances in a liquid, such as the pigments in inks and dyes. In the Separating Colors experiment on pp. 20–21, the pigments separate into their different colors, mainly because the ones made up of larger molecules move more slowly on paper, while others move faster and farther away.

**molecule:** All matter is made of atoms, and atoms combine with other atoms to form molecules. Some molecules are composed of the same atoms: for example, two atoms of oxygen make one molecule of oxygen. Other moelcules are composed of different atoms: one atom of oxygen and two atoms of hydrogen make one molecule of water.

**non-Newtonian fluid:** A Newtonian fluid (named after Sir Isaac Newton), such as water, changes shape according to the force applied to it, so a big force creates a big change in shape. Non-Newtonian fluids do not do this. Small forces cause them to change shape, but big forces do not. In the Cornstarch Slime experiment on p. 17, when a large force is applied to the slime, instead of flowing like a fluid, the substance behaves like a solid, going hard instead.

**Cartesian diver:** An experiment (pp. 8–9) to demonstrate the principle of buoyancy, in which the weight of an object immersed in water is opposed by an upward force exerted by the fluid. The upward force is equivalent to the weight of water displaced (pushed aside) by the object.

**oxidation:** The gaining of oxygen by a substance. The metal magnesium (used in fireworks) combines with oxygen to form magnesium oxide, which is used to make heat-resistant bricks. Iron combined with oxygen and water forms iron oxide, or rust.

# Did You Know?

* Water, a fluid, is made from two gases—hydrogen and oxygen. You can split it back into hydrogen and oxygen by passing electricity through it. This is called electrolysis. If those gases are mixed and set alight, you get an explosion and rainfall!

* Spies and prisoners have often written messages in invisible ink. During the American Revolutionary War, spies for George Washington supplied him with information about enemy movements by writing in invisible ink. The ink recipe was made for Washington by a doctor, and they called it "medicine." Spies also used a numerical code to write messages. Their activities were never discovered during the war.

* Aluminium oxide is naturally clear, but when mixed with impurities, it changes color to form beautiful and precious gemstones: blue for sapphires and red for rubies.

* The Statue of Liberty is covered in copper plating, which long ago turned green from its original orangey-red. The copper went through various chemical processes, first by oxidizing and then reacting with moisture and gases in the air to make the green layer we see today.

# INDEX

## The Author

Rob Ives is a former math and science teacher, now a designer and paper engineer living in Cumbria, UK. He creates science- and project-based children's books, including *Paper Models that Rock!* and *Paper Automata*. He specializes in character-based paper animations and all kinds of fun and fascinating science projects, and he often visits schools to talk about design technology and demonstrate his models.

## The Illustrator

Eva Sassin is a freelance illustrator born in London, UK. She has always loved illustrating, whether it be scary, fun monsters or cute, sparkly fairies. She carries a sketchbook everywhere, but she has even drawn on the back of receipts if she's forgotten it! In her free time, she travels around London to visit exhibitions and small cafés where she enjoys sketching up new ideas and characters. She is also a massive film buff!

**Picture Credits** (abbreviations: t = top; b = bottom; c = center; l = left; r = right)
© www.shutterstock.com:

9 br, 11 br, 13 br, 21 br, 22 bl, 23 br, 25 br, 27 br, 31 tl, 31 tr, 31 cr, 31 cl, 31 br.